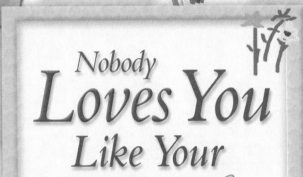

Nobody
Loves You
Like Your
Kids

for you mom

Nobody
Loves You
Like Your
Kids

New Leaf Press

First Printing: February 2004

Cover by RSWalch Design
Interior design by Brent Spurlock
Edited by Jim Fletcher and Roger Howerton

ISBN: 0-89221-566-6
Library of Congress Catalog Card Number: 2003116019

Please visit our web site for more great titles:
www.newleafpress.net

New Leaf Press

Printed in Italy

. . . for he hath said, I will never leave thee, nor forsake thee.

– Hebrews 13:5

A special gift for you

To

_____

From

_____

for you mom

INTRODUCTION

It's about relationships. How many times have you heard that? It's true, isn't it?

Life is very much tied to the relationships we have with people: family, friends, even enemies. Unless we live alone in a forest, we interact with other humans on a daily basis.

And because we are human, love becomes a huge part of our relationships. We crave it, nurture it, hope for it. For obvious reasons, those we live with are the recipients of varying degrees of love. A little one approaches because someone stepped on his finger during play-time. A phone call is about one sister needing another sister, right now. A plea from college gives a mom or dad the opportunity to "love on" a homesick freshman.

If life is beautiful, then love is its face. The stories and vignettes in this book are about people and their relationships with those they love. They'll make you feel good, maybe make you cry, maybe cause you to think a bit more about someone who needs you.

Even the lengths of these love reminders have been chosen with care: sometimes you need a quick pick-me-up, a short read. Sometimes you have the time, and perhaps the need, to curl up for awhile and read about the human relationship.

Wherever you are in your life journey, take time to pause and reflect. It's all about love; everything else is just noise. Because nobody loves you like your kids.

for you mom

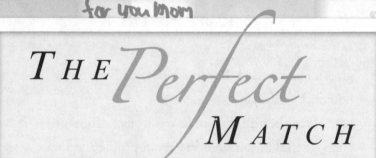

THE *Perfect* MATCH

I t had been a long day and
Debbie felt like going home and
falling into bed. The job was
too stressful, her car was making
funny noises, and something deep
inside whispered "ulcer."

Still, perhaps out of habit, she turned down
Cherry Street and headed for the high school soccer
field. Bone-tired, she plotted ways to leave Scott's
game early. The teen would understand, right? At least
Debbie would make an appearance.

Scott was different, in more ways than one. Born
early, his lungs were small, and something as routine
as soccer practice and matches became challenging. In
fact, the coach let him on the team out of pity, really.
Scott rarely played more than a minute or two.

He was also different in that his maturity was
more advanced than most kids his age. Never gave
his single mother any trouble. Debbie thought about
these things and smiled to herself as she pulled into
the parking lot. Dragging herself out of the car, she
heard the thumps and grunts of the game. The bleep
of her car-lock system seemed to increase the intensity

of her headache. Maybe she'd have some gooey nachos for dinner as she watched the match. . . .

The setting sun was met by the field lights. Something kept Debbie in her seat, although Scott was also warming his own seat. That's okay, thought Debbie, at least it gives him something to do.

The rapidly solidifying cheese in the plastic tray remained untouched as Debbie made small talk with several parents. She strained her eyes toward the field when someone elbowed her and pointed to Scott, who was pulling off his sweater. The slight teen jogged out onto the field and took his position.

Forty seconds. That's all Scott lasted before he became too winded to continue. He grinned and waved as he made his way back to the bench.

Afterward in the darkness of the car, Debbie half-listened as they drove home. Scott went on and

on about his day, just routine stuff. Then he said
something that Debbie still hears:

"Mom, I really appreciate you being there today. I
was so tired when the match started that I just wanted
to quit. But when I saw you, I didn't feel so tired. I
got to play; did you see me?"

Debbie looked at the highway, then looked at
Scott. She put a hand on his shoulder and squeezed.

"I did see you; I'm proud of you. I love you, too,
son."

---

*Suffer little children to come unto me, and
forbid them not: for of such is the kingdom of God*

– Luke 18:16

*While we try to teach our children all about life, our
children teach us what life is all about.*

– Angela Schwindt

IMPORTUNITY
Knocks

A small boy is sent to bed by his father. Five minutes later, he calls, "Da-ad. . . ."

"What?"

"I'm thirsty. Can you bring me a drink of water?"

"No. You had your chance. Lights out."

Five minutes later, "Da-aaaad . . ."

"WHAT?"

"I'm THIRSTY. Can I have a drink of water??"

"I told you NO! If you ask again, I'll have to spank you!!"

Five minutes later, "Daaaa-aaaad. . . ."

"WHAT??!!"

"When you come in to spank me, can you bring me a drink of water?"

> *Foolishness is bound in the heart of a child; but the rod of correction shall drive it far from him.*
> – Proverbs 22:15

SLEEPING *Beauty*

To Dad
I love You

ver notice how a four-year-old's voice is louder than 200 adult voices?

Several years ago, I returned home from a trip just when a storm hit, with crashing thunder and severe lightning. As I came into my bedroom about two a.m., I found my two children in bed with my wife, Karey, apparently scared by the loud storm. I resigned myself to sleep in the guest bedroom that night.

The next day, I talked to the children, and explained that it was OK to sleep with Mom when the storm was bad, but when I was expected home, please don't sleep with Mom that night. They said OK.

After my next trip several weeks later, Karey and the children picked me up in the terminal at the appointed time. Since the plane was late, everyone had come into the terminal to wait for my plane's arrival, along with hundreds of other folks waiting for their arriving passengers. As I entered the waiting area, my son saw me, and came running shouting, "Hi, Dad! I've got some good news!"

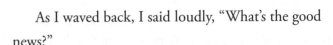

As I waved back, I said loudly, "What's the good news?"

"Nobody slept with Mommy while you were away this time!" Alex shouted.

The airport became very quiet, as everyone in the waiting area looked at Alex, then turned to me, and then searched the rest of the area to see if they could figure out exactly who his mom was.

> *Even a child is known by his doings, whether his work be pure, and whether it be right.*
>
> — Proverbs 20:11

for you mom

ARE YOU GOD'S *Wife?*

To Dad
I love You

little boy about ten years old was standing before a shoe store on the roadway, barefooted, peering through the window, and shivering with cold. A lady approached the boy and said, "My little fellow, why are you looking so earnestly in that window?"

"I was asking God to give me a pair of shoes," was the boy's reply.

The lady took him by the hand and went into the store and asked the clerk to get half a dozen pairs of socks for the boy. She then asked if he could give her a basin of water and a towel. He quickly brought them to her. She took the little guy to the back part of the store and removing her gloves, knelt down, washed his little feet, and dried them with a towel. By this time the clerk returned with the socks. Placing a pair upon the boy's feet, she purchased him a pair of shoes. She tied up the remaining pairs of socks and gave them to him. She patted him on the head and said, "No doubt, my little fellow, you feel more comfortable now?"

As she turned to go, the astonished lad caught her by the hand, and looking up in her face, said, "Are you God's wife?"

for you mom

OUT OF THE MOUTHS OF *Babes*

To Dad
I love you

woman was trying hard to get the
ketchup to come out of the bottle.
During her struggle, the phone
rang so she asked her four-year-

old daughter to answer the phone. "It's the minister, Mommy," the child said to her mother. Then she added, "Mommy can't come to the phone to talk to you right now. She's hitting the bottle."

"*A small child is someone who can wash his hands without getting the soap wet.*"
– Anonymous

A GOOD REASON TO GO TO *Church*

To Dad
I love you

I t was Palm Sunday and, because of a sore throat, five-year-old Johnny stayed home from church with a sitter. When the family returned home, they were carrying several palm branches.

The boy asked what they were for.

"People held them over Jesus' head as He walked by."

"Wouldn't you know it," the boy fumed, "the one Sunday I don't go, He shows up!"

> *And the multitudes that went before, and that followed, cried, saying, Hosanna to the Son of David: Blessed is he that cometh in the name of the Lord; Hosanna in the highest. And when he was come into Jerusalem, all the city was moved, saying, Who is this? And the multitude said, This is Jesus the prophet of Nazareth of Galilee.*
> — Matthew 21: 9-11

D ear GOD, Thank you for the baby brother, but what I prayed for was a puppy.

– Joyce

Delight thyself also in the LORD; and he shall give thee the desires of thine heart.

– Psalm 37:4

YOU KNOW IT'S
FROM THE *Heart*

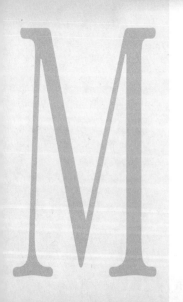

My youngest son is the third of three boys. The first two are high-powered; the third is not any less high-powered, but he's the third out of three. By the time you've had a brother who's all-conference this and another brother who's all-conference that, there's not much left for you to do.

As a father, I worried about our caboose. He is the most sensitive of the three. To encourage him, I spent a lot of time with him in the outdoors — camping, hunting, fishing. Anybody who has spent time in the outdoors knows that a pocketknife is essential gear — the man with the best blade gets the job done. So, whenever you're setting up camp, you're always looking for the knife.

My son Ryan had a pocketknife that became his identity. His older brothers always had to ask him to use the knife as we were setting up camp. That became his status in the tribe. He was the man with the blade.

My birthday came around one year, and my

family was planning a party for me. Earlier in the afternoon, my youngest walked into my office at home where I was studying. At first I didn't hear him; I felt him — I could sense his presence — and I turned around.

He had chosen this moment because he wanted to give me a birthday present but not at the birthday party. He wanted it to be just me and him. He handed me a present, and I opened it — it was his knife.[1]

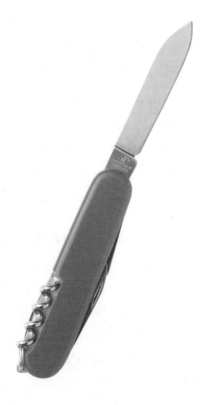

JUST *Ask* A CHILD

A first grade teacher collected well known proverbs. She gave each kid in the class the first half of the proverb, and asked them to come up with the rest. Here is what the kids came up with:

Better to be safe than.......punch a 5th grader.

Strike while the........................bug is close.

It's always darkest before..............daylight
savings time.

Never underestimate the power of............termites.

You can lead a horse to water but ....how?

Don't bite the hand that...............looks dirty.

No news is........................impossible.

A miss is as good as a........................Mr.

You can't teach an old dog...................math.

If you lie down with dogs, you........will stink
in the morning.

Love all, trust.......................me.

The pen is mightier than..................the pigs.

An idle mind is............the best way to relax.

Where there is smoke, there's.........pollution.

Happy is the bride who.................gets
all the presents.

A penny saved is.........................not much.

Two is company, three's....................the Musketeers.

None are so blind as.................Helen Keller.

Children should be seen and not..........spanked or
    grounded.

If at first you don't succeed.................get new
    batteries.

You get out of something what you.......see pictured
    on the box.

When the blind lead the blind................get out
    of the way.

There is no fool like......................Aunt Edie.

Laugh and the whole world laughs with you.
    Cry and.......you have to blow your nose.

for you mom

S

he was six years old when I first met her on the beach near where I live. I drive to this beach, a distance of three or four miles, whenever the world begins to close in on me.

To Dad
I love You

She was building a sand castle or something and looked up, her eyes blue as the sea.

"Hello," she said.

I answered with a nod, not really in the mood to bother with a small child.

"I'm building," she said.

"I see that. What is it?" I asked, not caring.

"Oh, I don't know, I just like the feel of the sand."

That sounds good, I thought, and slipped off my shoes. A sandpiper glided by.

"That's a joy," the child said.

"It's what?" I asked, uncaring.

"It's a joy! My mama says sandpipers come to bring us joy."

The bird went gliding down the beach. "Good-bye joy," I muttered to myself, "Hello, pain . . ." and turned to walk on. I was depressed; my life seemed completely out of balance.

"What's your name?" She wouldn't give up.

"Ruth," I answered. "I'm Ruth Peterson."

"Mine's Wendy, ... and I'm six."

"Hi, Wendy," I offered.

She giggled. "You're funny," she said. In spite of my gloom I laughed too and walked on. Her musical giggle followed me. "Come again, Mrs. P." she called. "We'll have another happy day."

The days and weeks that followed belonged to others: a group of unruly Boy Scouts, PTA meetings, an ailing mother. The sun was shining one morning as I took my hands out of the dishwater.

"I need a sandpiper," I said to myself, gathering up my coat.

The never-changing balm of the seashore awaited me. The breeze was chilly, but I strode along, trying to recapture the serenity I needed. I had forgotten the child and was startled when she appeared.

"Hello, Mrs. P." she said. "Do you want to play?"

"What did you have in mind?" I asked, with a twinge of annoyance.

"I don't know. You say."

"How about charades?" I asked sarcastically.

The tinkling laughter burst forth again. "I don't know what that is."

"Then let's just walk." Looking at her, I noticed the delicate fairness of her face.

"Where do you live?" I asked.

"Over there." She pointed toward a row of summer cottages. Strange, I thought, in winter.

"Where do you go to school?"

"I don't go to school. Mommy says we're on vacation."

She chattered little girl talk as we strolled up the beach, but my mind was on other things. "When I left for home," Wendy said, "it had been a happy day."

Feeling surprisingly better, I smiled at her and agreed.

Three weeks later, I rushed to my beach in a state of near panic. I was in no mood to greet even Wendy. I thought I saw her mother on the porch and felt like demanding she keep her child at home.

"Look, if you don't mind," I said crossly when Wendy caught up with me, "I'd rather be alone today." She seemed unusually pale and out of breath.

"Why?" she asked.

I turned on her and shouted, "Because my mother died!" and thought . . . *why was I saying this to a little child?*

"Oh," she said quietly, "then this is a bad day."

"Yes, and yesterday and the day before that and — oh, go away!"

"Did it hurt?"

"Did what hurt?" I was exasperated with her, with myself.

"When she died?"

"Of course it hurt!" I snapped, misunderstanding, wrapped up in myself. I strode off.

A month or so after that, when I next went to the beach, she wasn't there.

Feeling guilty, ashamed and admitting to myself I missed her, I went up to the cottage after my walk and knocked at the door. A drawn-looking young woman with honey-colored hair opened the door.

"Hello," I said. "I'm Ruth Peterson. I missed your little girl today and wondered where she was."

"Oh yes, Mrs. Peterson, please come in. Wendy talked of you so much. I'm afraid I allowed her to bother you. If she was a nuisance, please accept my apologies."

"Not at all — she's a delightful child," I said, suddenly realizing that I meant it. "Where is she?"

"Wendy died last week, Mrs. Peterson. She had leukemia. Maybe she didn't tell you."

Struck dumb, I groped for a chair. My breath caught.

"She loved this beach; so when she asked to come, we couldn't say no. She seemed so much better here and had a lot of what she called happy days. But the last few weeks, she declined rapidly . . ." Her voice faltered.

"She left something for you . . . if only I can find it. Could you wait a moment while I look?"

I nodded stupidly, my mind racing for something, anything, to say to this lovely young woman.

She handed me a smeared envelope, with "MRS. P." printed in bold, childish letters. Inside was a drawing in bright crayon hues — a yellow beach, a blue sea, a brown bird. Underneath was carefully printed: "A SANDPIPER TO BRING YOU JOY."

Tears welled up in my eyes, and a heart that had almost forgotten how to love opened wide. I took Wendy's mother in my arms. "I'm sorry, I'm sorry,

I'm so sorry," I muttered over and over, and we wept together.

The precious little picture is framed now and hangs in my study. Six words — one for each year of her life — that speak to me of inner harmony, courage, undemanding love. A gift from a child with sea — blue eyes and hair the color of sand — who taught me the gift of love.[2]

Dear GOD, I didn't think orange went with purple until I saw the sunset you made on Tuesday. That was cool!

– Eugene

O magnify the LORD with me, and let us exalt his name together.

– Psalm 34:3

CHILD'S
Admission

A little boy in church for the first time watched as the ushers took up the collection. When they came near his pew, the boy said loudly, "Don't pay for me, Daddy. I'm under five."

Dear GOD, I went to this wedding and they kissed right in church. Is that okay?

– Neil (age 7)

Trick QUESTION

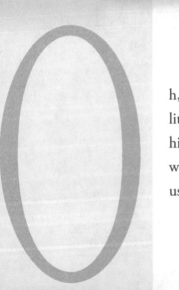

"Oh, I sure am happy to see you," the little boy said to his grandmother on his mother's side. "Now maybe Daddy will do the trick he has been promising us."

The grandmother was curious.

"What trick is that?" she asked. "I heard him tell Mommy that he would climb the walls if you came to visit," the little boy answered.

Dear GOD, My brother told me about being born but it doesn't sound right. They're just kidding, aren't they?

– Marsha

PRECAUTIONARY *Prayer*

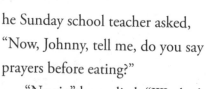

The Sunday school teacher asked, "Now, Johnny, tell me, do you say prayers before eating?"

"No sir," he replied, "We don't have to. My mom is a good cook!"

Dear GOD, Why is Sunday school on Sunday? I thought it was supposed to be our day of rest.

– Tom

JUST LIKE *Dad*

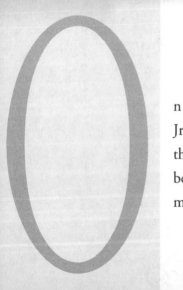

O n September 6, 1995, Cal Ripken,
Jr. broke the baseball record
that many believed would never
be broken: Lou Gehrig's iron-
man feat of playing in 2,131

consecutive games. Ripken gives much of the credit
for his accomplishments to the example and teaching
of his father, Cal Ripken, Sr., who played minor
league baseball, and coached and managed for the
Orioles.

During the 1996 season, Ripken, Sr. was inducted
into the Orioles Hall of Fame. After he gave his
acceptance speech, the son came to the microphone,
an emotional moment recalled in his book, *The Only
Way I Know:*

>It was difficult. I wasn't certain I could say
>what I wanted about my father and what he
>means to me. So I told a little story about my
>two children, Rachel, six at the time, and Ryan,
>then three. They'd been bickering for weeks, and I
>explained how one day I heard Rachel taunt Ryan,
>"You're just trying to be like Daddy."

After a few moments of indecision, I asked Rachel, "What's wrong with trying to be like Dad?"

When I finished telling the story, I looked at my father and added, "That's what I've always tried to do."[3]

for you mom

Righting
A SERMON

A boy was watching his father, a
pastor, write a sermon. "How do
you know what to say?" he asked.

"Why, God tells me," the father replied.

"Oh, then why do you keep crossing things out?"

Improving
OVER TIME

To Dad
I love You

little girl was sitting on her grandfather's lap as he read her a bedtime story. From time to time, she would take her eyes off the book and reach up to touch his wrinkled cheek.

She was alternately stroking her own cheek, then his again. Finally she spoke up, "Grandpa, did God make you?"

"Yes, sweetheart," he answered, "God made me a long time ago."

"Oh," she paused, "Grandpa, did God make me too?"

"Yes, indeed, honey," he said, "God made you just a little while ago."

Feeling their respective faces again, she observed, "God's getting better at it, isn't He?"

> *Children's children are the crown of old men; and the glory of children are their fathers.*
>
> – Proverbs 17:6

SAFETY *First*

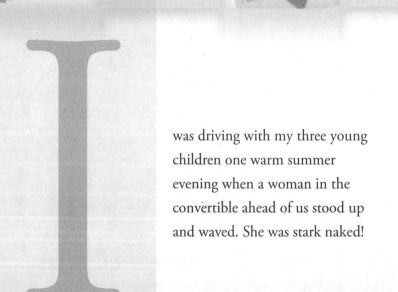

I was driving with my three young children one warm summer evening when a woman in the convertible ahead of us stood up and waved. She was stark naked!

As I was reeling from the shock, I heard my five-year-old shout from the back seat, "Mom! That lady isn't wearing a seat belt!"

A child is a person who can't understand why some would give away a perfectly good kitten.

Wrong ADDRESS

After the christening of his baby brother in church, little Johnny sobbed all the way home in the back seat of the car. His father asked him three times what was wrong. Finally, the boy replied, "That priest said he wanted us brought up in a Christian home, and I want to stay with you guys!"

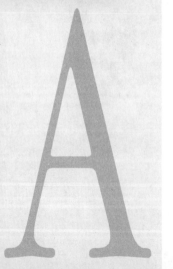

for you mom

WHAT IS A
Grandmother

A n eight year old wrote, "A grandmother is a lady who has no children of her own, so she likes other people's boys and girls. Grandmas don't have anything to do except be there. If they take us for walks, they slow down past pretty leaves and caterpillars. They never say 'Hurry up.' Usually they are fat but not too fat to tie shoes. They wear glasses, and sometimes they can take their teeth out. They can answer questions like why dogs hate cats and why God isn't married. When they read to us, they don't skip words or mind if it is the same story again. Everybody should try to have a grandma, especially if you don't have television, because grandmas are the only grownups who always have time."

Age–
OLD QUESTION

ittle Johnny asked his grandmother
how old she was. Grandma
answered, "Thirty-nine and
holding."

Johnny thought for a moment, and then said, "And how old would you be if you let go?"

for you mom

CHRISTMAS *Love*

Each December, I vowed to make Christmas a calm and peaceful experience. I had cut back on nonessential obligations — extensive card writing, endless baking, decorating, and even overspending. Yet still, I found

myself exhausted, unable to appreciate the precious
family moments, and of course, the true meaning of
Christmas.

My son, Nicholas, was in kindergarten that year.
It was an exciting season for a six year old. For weeks,
he'd been memorizing songs for his school's "Winter
Pageant."

I didn't have the heart to tell him I'd be working
the night of the production. Unwilling to miss his
shining moment, I spoke with his teacher. She assured
me there'd be a dress rehearsal the morning of the
presentation. All parents unable to attend that evening
were welcome to come then. Fortunately, Nicholas
seemed happy with the compromise.

So, the morning of the dress rehearsal, I filed in
ten minutes early, found a spot on the cafeteria floor
and sat down. Around the room, I saw several other

parents quietly scampering to their seats. As I waited, the students were led into the room. Each class, accompanied by their teacher, sat cross-legged on the floor. Then, each group, one by one, rose to perform their song. Because the public school system had long stopped referring to the holiday as "Christmas," I didn't expect anything other than fun, commercial entertainment — songs of reindeer, Santa Claus, snowflakes, and good cheer.

So, when my son's class rose to sing, "Christmas Love," I was slightly taken aback by its bold title. Nicholas was aglow, as were all of his classmates, adorned in fuzzy mittens, red sweaters, and bright snowcaps upon their heads. Those in the front row, center stage, held up large letters, one by one, to spell out the title of the song.

As the class would sing "C is for Christmas," a

child would hold up the letter C. Then, "H is for happy," and on and on, until each child holding up his portion had presented the complete message, "Christmas Love."

The performance was going smoothly, until suddenly, we noticed her — a small, quiet, girl in the front row holding the letter "M" upside down — totally unaware her letter "M" appeared as a "W."

The audience of first through sixth graders snickered at this little one's mistake. But she had no idea they were laughing at her, so she stood tall, proudly holding her "W."

Although many teachers tried to shush the children, the laughter continued until the last letter was raised, and we all saw it together. A hush came over the audience and eyes began to widen. In that instant, we understood — the reason we were there,

why we celebrated the holiday in the first place;
why even in the chaos, there was a purpose for our
festivities.

For when the last letter was held high, the message
read loud and clear:

"CHRIST WAS LOVE."
And I believe He still is!

For God sent not his Son into the world to condemn the world; but that the world through him might be saved.

– John 3:17

WELL *Almost*

A six year old was overheard reciting the Lord's Prayer at a church service: "And forgive us our trash passes, as we forgive those who passed trash against us."

Whosoever therefore shall humble himself as this little child, the same is greatest in the kingdom of heaven.

– Matthew 18:4

GONE TO *Heaven*

To Dad
I love You

A father was at the beach with his children when the four-year-old son ran up to him, grabbed his hand, and led him to the shore, where a seagull lay dead in the sand. "Daddy, what happened to him?" the son asked.

"He died and went to heaven," the dad replied.

The boy thought a moment and then said, "Did God throw him back down?"

> *Hear, ye children, the instruction of a father, and attend to know understanding.*
>
> — Proverbs 4:1

for you mom

WHAT'S THE *Hubbub?*

To Dad
I love You

A little boy got lost at the YMCA
and found himself in the women's
locker room. When he was spotted,
the room burst into shrieks, with

ladies grabbing towels and running for cover. The little boy watched in amazement and then asked, "What's the matter? Haven't you ever seen a little boy before?"

D ear GOD, Who draws the lines around the countries?

– Nan

As Long As You Need Me

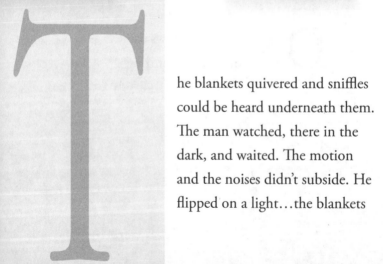

T

he blankets quivered and sniffles could be heard underneath them. The man watched, there in the dark, and waited. The motion and the noises didn't subside. He flipped on a light…the blankets were still. All was quiet, except the sound of the man's shoes on the wood floor.

Reaching the bed, he sat down and put his hand on a shock of hair that peeked out from the blanket, which sported one of those happy Disney characters. The little boy under the blanket, however, was not happy.

"Tell Dad what's wrong," the man said.

"N-nothing," whispered the little boy.

"Well, it must be something," he soothed. "I think you should tell me."

The boy hesitated, wise enough to understand that his father had many responsibilities. He was surely tired and wanted to go to bed himself. A gentle squeeze prompted the son to let the emotional dam break.

"I miss Mom!" he wailed.

The father, choked with his own feelings, pulled the little boy close and rocked him back and forth. "I know" was all he said for some time. The boy's sobs echoed off the bedroom walls. Nearby, a clock ticked and ticked. Continuing to rock, the father began.

"I know you miss her. I do, too." He was almost whispering.

"You know," he continued, "she didn't want to leave, and we mustn't be mad at God for taking her."

A pair of wet, red eyes looked into his.

"I know, Daddy. I'm not mad at God."

"So you're just sad?"

The tears spilled out again.

"That's not all, Daddy. I'm afraid you'll die, too!"

So that was it. The father thought quickly. He hugged his son.

"I'll tell you what, I promise that I'll be with you as long as you need me."

Even though the night was dark, the sun came out, if just a little, in their hearts. The boy fell asleep, content, in his father's arms.

Years passed. One day, a still-handsome grandfather heard the phone ringing. He put down his pruning shears and hurried inside.

"Dad? I-I just wanted to let you know that we lost the baby. No, Erica's fine. I just wanted to talk to you. Pretty silly, huh? I'm a grown man!"

"Son, there's nothing wrong with needing to talk. I'll tell you what, I promise that I'll be with you as long as you need me."

One winter day, the hospice worker moved away, discreetly slipping out the door. A middle-aged man watched an old man. The latter gasped once or twice,

then opened his eyes. A puzzled look glided over his tired face. Perhaps it was a little bit of fear.

The younger man stood up, stiffly. It had been a long night. He took a step toward the bed and let down the guard rail. Sinking gently into the sheets, he looked into the eyes of his father. Carefully, he slipped an arm under the thin torso and lifted. He wiped perspiration from the wrinkled brow. Rocking back and forth, his eyes moist, he whispered:

"I'll tell you what, I promise that I'll be with you as long as you need me."

There, in the still room, a clock ticked and ticked. The sun slipped through the shadows and spread over the bed and warmed the two still figures.

But the mercy of the LORD is from everlasting to everlasting upon them that fear him, and his righteousness unto children's children.

– Psalm 103:17

Unbelievable

While working for an organization that delivers lunches to elderly shut-ins, I used to take my four-year-old daughter on my afternoon rounds. She was unfailingly intrigued by the various appliances of old age, particularly the canes, walkers and wheelchairs. One day I found her staring at a pair of false teeth soaking in a glass. As I braced myself for the inevitable barrage of questions, she merely turned and whispered, "The tooth fairy will never believe this!"

> *Verily I say unto you, Whosoever shall not receive the kingdom of God as a little child shall in no wise enter therein.*
>
> – Luke 18:17

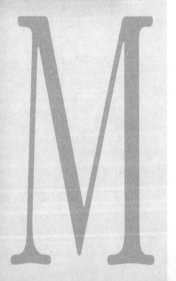

for you mom

"SUSTAINING Mom"

om, I need a hug." My 12-year-old daughter stood beside me, blinking tears.

"Whatever is the matter?" I said, putting my arm around her.

"I can't bear the thought of losing Riley someday," she choked.

I hugged her tightly. I knew the issue was more than the fear over the death of our old dog. Our family had faced multiple losses over the past year, including the death of my grandmother and the loss of my husband's job. His new job out of state meant losing friends and our beautiful home. We had just received word that week that our house had finally sold, yet the sale signified another loss to Alison.

"How can I help you feel better?" Surprised at how my words showed my own sense of loss, I prayed for wisdom I didn't have. Alison gave me my starting line.

"Tell me what you always tell me, Mom — that God is in control."

"More than that, honey. He cares about you too.
Look how He has been constantly with us even when
we didn't know when Dad would get a new job.
He has provided everything we need at exactly the
right time. God will give you the strength you need
when it's time for Riley to go, and He will not allow
anything to happen that you can't handle."

She gave me a shaky smile and walked away.
Half an hour later, she returned my hug. "Thanks
for reminding me of those things," she said. "I
remembered that psalm you made us memorize when
we were kids — the one that says He never sleeps
or slumbers, God will always be with us, no matter
what."

It was my turn to smile. "You know, honey,
remembering what God has done is like saying thank

You to Him. And it always helps to thank and praise Him."

> *Draw nigh to God, and he will draw nigh to you. . . .*
> — James 4:8

for you mom

Disclaimer

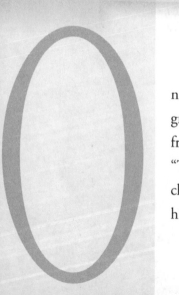

On the first day of school, a first-grader handed his teacher a note from his mother. The note read, "The opinions expressed by this child are not necessarily those of his parents."

Dear GOD, We read Thomas Edison made light. But in school they said You did it. So I bet he stoled your idea.

– Sincerely, Donna

WHAT A TOUGH *Job*

To Dad
I love you

hen my daughter was about seven years old, she asked me one day what I did at work. I told her I worked at the college — that my job was to teach people how to draw. She stared at me, incredulous, and said, "You mean they forget?"[4]

> *If thy children will keep my covenant and my testimony that I shall teach them, their children shall also sit upon thy throne for evermore.*
>
> – Psalm 132:12

for you mom

WHEN YOU THOUGHT I *Wasn't* LOOKING
(WRITTEN BY A FORMER CHILD)

A message every adult should read, because children are watching you and doing as you do, not as you say.

When you thought I wasn't looking, I saw you hang my first painting on the refrigerator, and I immediately wanted to paint another one.

When you thought I wasn't looking I saw you feed a stray cat, and I learned that it was good to be kind to animals.

When you thought I wasn't looking, I saw you make my favorite cake for me and I learned that the little things can be the special things in life.

When you thought I wasn't looking I heard you

say a prayer, and I knew there is a God I could always talk to and I learned to trust in God.

When you thought I wasn't looking, I saw you make a meal and take it to a friend who was sick, and I learned that we all have to help take care of each other.

When you thought I wasn't looking, I saw you give of your time and money to help people who had nothing and I learned that those who have something should give to those who don't.

When you thought I wasn't looking, I saw you take care of our house and everyone in it and I learned we have to take care of what we are given.

When you thought I wasn't looking, I saw how you handled your responsibilities, even when you didn't feel good and I learned that I would have to be responsible when I grow up.

When you thought I wasn't looking, I saw tears come from your eyes and I learned that sometimes things hurt, but it's all right to cry.

When you thought I wasn't looking, I saw that you cared and I wanted to be everything that I could be.

When you thought I wasn't looking, I learned most of life's lessons that I need to know to be a good and productive person when I grow up.

When you thought I wasn't looking, I looked at you and wanted to say, "Thanks for all the things I saw when you thought I wasn't looking."

Train up a child in the way he should go: and when he is old, he will not depart from it.

– Proverbs 22:6

Dear GOD, Maybe Cain and Abel would not kill each other so much if they had their own rooms. It works with my brother.

– Larry

How excellent is thy lovingkindness, O God!
therefore the children of men put their trust
under the shadow of thy wings.

– Psalm 36:7

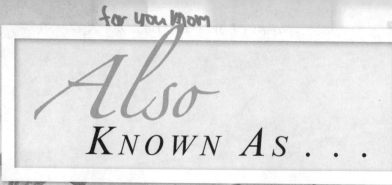

for you mom

Also
KNOWN AS . . . .

To Dad
I love You

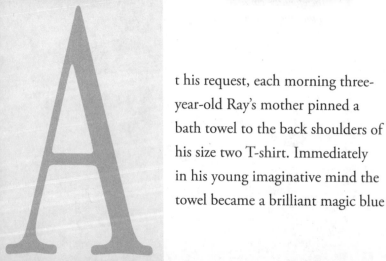

A

t his request, each morning three-
year-old Ray's mother pinned a
bath towel to the back shoulders of
his size two T-shirt. Immediately
in his young imaginative mind the
towel became a brilliant magic blue

and red cape and he became Superman. Outfitted each day in his "cape," Ray's days were packed with adventure and daring escapades. He was Superman.

This fact was clearly pointed out last fall when his mother enrolled him in kindergarten class. During the course of the interview, the teacher asked Ray his name.

"Superman," he answered politely and without pause.

The teacher smiled, cast an appreciative glance at his mother, and asked again, "Your real name, please."

Again, Ray answered, "Superman."

Realizing the situation demanded more authority, or maybe to hide amusement, the teacher closed her eyes for a moment, then in a voice quite stern, said, "I will have to have your real name for the records."

Sensing he'd have to play straight with the teacher,

Ray slid his eyes around the room, hunched closer
to her, and patting a corner of frayed towel at his
shoulder, answered in a voice hushed with conspiracy,
"Clark Kent."

Dear GOD, Please send me a pony. I
never asked for anything before, You can
look it up.

– Bruce

for you mom

Helping
HAND

hile taking a routine vandalism report at an elementary school, I was interrupted by a little girl about six years old. Looking up and down at my uniform, she asked, "Are you a cop?"

"Yes," I answered and continued writing the report.

"My mother said if I ever needed

help I should ask the police. Is that right?"

"Yes, that's right," I told her.

"Well, then," she said as she extended her foot toward me, "would you please tie my shoe?"

A little girl had just finished her first week of school. "I'm just wasting my time," she said to her mother. "I can't read, I can't write, and they won't let me talk!"

THE *Best* PART OF WAKING UP

A sweet little boy surprised his grandmother one morning and brought her a cup of coffee. He made it himself and was so proud. He anxiously waited to hear the verdict on the quality of the coffee. The grandmother had never in her life had such a bad cup of coffee, and as she forced down the last sip she noticed three of those little green army guys in the bottom of the cup.

She asked, "Honey, why would three little green army guys be in the bottom of my cup?"

Her grandson replied, "You know Grandma, it's like on TV, 'The best part of waking up is soldiers in your cup.'"

WHO'S TESTING *Whom?*

I didn't know if my granddaughter had learned her colors yet, so I decided to test her. I would point out something and ask her what color it was. She would tell me and always she was correct. But it was fun for me, so I continued. At last she headed for the door, saying sagely, "Grandma, I think you should try to figure out some of these yourself."

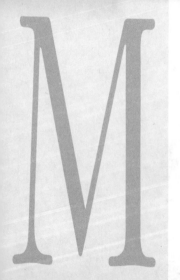

for you mom

Honesty
IS THE BEST POLICY

M y four-year-old son, Zachary, came
screaming out of the bathroom
to tell me he'd dropped his
toothbrush in the toilet. So I
fished it out and threw it in the
garbage. Zachary stood there

thinking for a moment, then ran to my bathroom and came out with my toothbrush. He held it up and said with a charming little smile, "We better throw this one out too then, cause it fell in the toilet a few days ago."

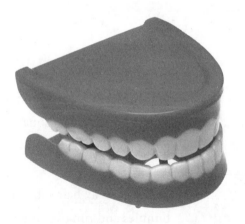

THINGS I'VE
Learned
FROM MY CHILDREN

To Dad
I love You

1

A king-size waterbed holds enough
water to fill a 2,000-square-foot
house four inches deep.

2. If you spray hair spray on dust
bunnies and run over them with
roller blades, they can ignite.

3. A three year old's voice is louder than 200 adults in a crowded restaurant.

4. If you hook a dog leash over a ceiling fan, the motor is not strong enough to rotate a 42-pound boy wearing Batman underwear and a Superman cape. It is strong enough, however, if tied to a paint can, to spread paint on all four walls of a 20-by-20-foot room.

5. You should not throw baseballs up when the ceiling fan is on. When using the ceiling fan as a bat, you have to throw the ball up a few times before you get a hit. A ceiling fan can hit a baseball a long way.

6. The glass in windows (even double pane) doesn't stop a baseball hit by a ceiling fan.

7. When you hear the toilet flush and the words "Uh-oh," it's already too late.

8. Brake fluid mixed with Clorox makes smoke, and lots of it.

9. A six year old can start a fire with a flint rock even though a 36-year-old man says they can only do it in the movies. A magnifying glass can start a fire even on an overcast day.

10. Certain Legos will pass through the digestive tract of a four year old.

11. "Play Dough" and "microwave" should never be used in the same sentence.

12. Super glue is forever.

13. No matter how much Jell-O you put in a swimming pool you still can't walk on water.

14. Pool filters do not like Jell-O.

15. VCR's do not eject PB&J sandwiches even though TV commercials show they do.

16. Garbage bags do not make good parachutes.

17. Marbles in gas tanks make lots of noise when driving.

18. No, you probably do not want to know what that odor is.

19. Always look in the oven before you turn it on. Plastic toys do not like ovens.

20. The fire department in Austin, Texas, has a five-minute response time.

21. The spin cycle on the washing machine does not make earthworms dizzy.

22. It will, however, make cats dizzy.

23. Cats throw up twice their body weight when dizzy.

TELLTALE SIGNS OF

Advanced

PARENTHOOD

To Dad
I love You

You count the sprinkles on each kid's cupcake to make sure they're equal.

You only have time to shave one leg at a time.

You hide in the bathroom just to get some "alone time."

You consider finger paint to be a controlled substance.

You've mastered the art of placing large amounts of scrambled eggs and pancakes on the same plate without anything "touching."

You hope ketchup is a vegetable because it's the only one your child eats.

You con your kid into thinking that "Toys R Us" is a toy MUSEUM and not really a store.

You fast-forward through the scene where Bambi's mom gets killed.

You hear YOUR parent's voice when it's you that screams, "Not in THOSE clothes you don't!"

You hire a sitter because the two of you haven't been out in ages, then spend half the night calling home to check on the kids.

You start offering to cut up other people's food for them!

A *Big* HELP

To Dad
I love you

As the mother looked out the window, she noticed Mrs. Martin's rocking chair on the porch. "That ol' rocking chair looks so lonely with Mrs. Martin gone. She was an awfully good neighbor and we'll miss her," she said.

Little Roger spoke up and told his mommy he was going to go see Mr. Martin. His mother discouraged little Roger, trying to explain it was too soon after Mrs. Martin's death.

Little Roger replied, "But Mommy, I'm a big help to Mr. Martin."

"How are you a big help Roger?" she asked.

Little Roger proudly smiled and said, "I help Mr. Martin cry!"

FINDING A *Voice*

(How Finding a Banana Split Made One Mom's Dream Come True) *by Terri Goggin*

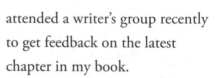

I attended a writer's group recently to get feedback on the latest chapter in my book.

There were so many people there that evening that discussion was limited. When I arrived home, my 13-year-old son shrugged off my disappointment and asked me to read the chapter to him instead. So I settled into a chair and read, "Down the Avenue," a chapter about spending my allowance as a nine-year-old child.

As innocent as it seems, the experience was a metaphor for how choice and risk were handled by a child affected by alcoholism. Each week, the trip "down-the-avenue" culminated at Woolworth's lunch counter, where I dreamed of someday ordering a banana split.

An umbrella with colorful balloons hanging from each rib was suspended above the counter. "Pop a balloon and pay 1 cent to 63 cents!" Imagine paying one cent for a banana split! But I never had more than 50 cents. And I shuddered at the thought

of Woolworth's calling my parents for more money. So I kept my wish to myself. I never thought to risk asking anyone for more money. Risks were dangerous in a world where alcohol made even benign choices subject to rage.

Frankie sat at my feet, listening intently, as I read the final sentences of the chapter:

I watched as others selected a balloon to pop and fantasized about the opportunity to proudly take my chance. But it never happened. Pink, blue, orange, and yellow balloons called out to me, daring me, taunting me, and eventually, defeating me. In time, the waitress strolled up to my spot at the counter and smiled, indicating that she was ready to jot down my order. I mumbled, "I'll take a Coke please," and turned the stool away from the umbrella. I didn't hear the sound of balloons popping behind me.

Frankie was silent. He thought for a moment and said, "So you never got the banana split?" A long discussion ensued, and eventually he seemed to understand that it was my own belief that limited me. I never took the chance of voicing my wish. It was a pattern that took years to break.

The next morning, Frankie casually announced that he was going out for a little while. When I asked where, he smiled and said, "I can't say. But when I get back, I'll need you to go upstairs for a few minutes." Any further questions of mine were answered with a coy, "You'll see."

My mother's instinct told me he wasn't up to anything dangerous, so I agreed. Frankie left, and I busied myself packing for an upcoming camping trip.

In a short time, I heard the back door open and Frankie's voice yelling, "Can you go upstairs now?" As I walked up the steps, I went through a mental checklist. *Hmm, it's not my birthday; it's not Mother's Day — what could he be up to?* I brushed my hair and tried to ignore the sound of chairs scraping, kitchen cabinets slamming, and muffled conversation. Soon my nine-year-old daughter Sarah, a last-minute recruit into the conspiracy, announced through giggles that I could come downstairs. "Eyes closed — except for stairs," she said.

Once downstairs, Sarah held my hand and helped me stumble my way through camping equipment and eventually into the kitchen.

"Open your eyes!" Frankie and Sarah shouted in chorus.

I couldn't believe what I saw. The kitchen table was covered in a pile of balloons. Frankie walked up to me and handed me 50 cents and a fork. His eyes were lit with anticipation. "Pop one!" he urged.

Tears welled up in my eyes as I began to realize what he was doing. I stared at the balloons in disbelief and then jabbed one with a fork. Frankie and Sarah laughed as I let out a loud whoop when it popped. A piece of paper fell out of the balloon. I opened it and recognized Frankie's awkward scrawl.

"What does it say?" Frankie prompted. "Fifty cents," I whispered, too choked up to speak loudly. Frankie got business-like and asked, "Well, do you have 50 cents?" I handed him the two quarters he'd given me moments earlier.

"OK then!" Frankie walked over to the refrigerator, pulled out a homemade banana split on a Tupperware plate, and handed it to me. Mounds of vanilla ice cream were covered in chocolate sauce, Cool Whip, and peanuts. Underneath it all was a banana, split in two. My eyes stung with tears as I held the banana split Frankie lovingly made to right an ancient wrong. I hugged Frankie hard and kissed the top of his head, still sweaty from all the effort.

"Now you finally got to pop a balloon for a banana split, Mom."

Frankie beamed. I hugged him again, and then

hugged Sarah, who stood back and marveled at her brother. We took turns popping the rest of the balloons and laughed when I finally got the 1-cent balloon. It was a long time coming but well worth the wait.

Each spoonful of ice cream reminded me that the first step in making any wish come true is giving it a voice.[5]

"Dear Pastor: My mother is very religious. She goes to play bingo at church every week even if she has a cold. Yours truly, Annette."

– Age 9, Albany

for you mom

Our pastor at Christ Lutheran Church, Long Beach, Calif.,
was telling the story of the wedding at Cana. After he told
how Jesus turned water into wine, he asked if anyone knew
what that was called. Without hesitation, one little charmer
blurted out: "Recycling."

— Margaret Madsen

Anaheim, Calif.

During a service at Redeemer Lutheran Church, Fort Myers, Fla., the pastor held up a bunch of keys. I believe he was going to tell about the keys to heaven. He asked the children what the keys were for. Some said to get into their home, unlock a cabinet, start the car, etc. Then a girl shouted, "Oh no, you don't need a key to start a car. My father can start one with a screwdriver."

– Einar M. Cannelin
Indianhead Park, Ill.

REFERENCES

[1] Craig Larson, *750 Engaging Stories for Preachers, Teachers, and Writers* (Grand Rapids, MI: Baker Books, 2003) p. 238, quoting from Stu Weber, "Whatever It Takes To Reach Men," *Leadership,* Fall 1994.

[2] Ruth Peterson, collected on the Internet

[3] Larson, *750 Engaging Stories for Preachers, Teachers, and Writers* (Grand Rapids, MI: Baker Books, 2003), quoting from Cal Ripken, Jr. and Mike Bryan, *The Only Way I Know* (New York: Viking, 1997)

[4] Howard Ikemoto

[5] Teri Goggin, Belief.net

Photo Credits

Babies (Comstock)

Childhood (Digital Vision) 19, 103

Dore Bible Illustrations (Dover)

Family Adventure (Eyewire) 57

Family Time (Eyewire) 47, 65

Friends (PhotoDisc) 5.

Generations (Thinkstock) 45, 69

Bryan Miller

Objectgear (Image Club) 23, 31, 117

Object Series: Moments in Life (PhotoDisk) 109, 115, 127

People & Pets (Eyewire) 26, 123

Scenic America (Dynamic Graphics) 6

Secondary Education 2 (Corbis) 59

Teens and Young Adults (Rubber Ball)